WORKSHOP MODELS FOR FAMILY LIFE EDUCATION

PARENTING CHILDREN OF DIVORCE

Peter Barnett
Christine P. Gaudio
Margaret G. Sumner

Family Service Association of America
44 East 23rd Street
New York, New York 10010

Library of Congress Cataloging in Publication Data

Barnett, Peter.
  Parenting children of divorce

  (Workshop models for family life education)
  Bibliography: p.
  1. Children of Divorced parents--Study and
teaching--United States. 2. Family life education
--curricula. 1. Gaudio, Christine P., joint
author. II. Sumner, Margaret G., joint author.
III. Title. IV. Series.
HQ777.5.B37   306.8'9   80-11044
ISBN 0-87304-178-X

Printed in the U.S.A.

Workshop Models for Family Life Education is a series of manuals intended to promote the exploration of new alternatives and the utilization of new options in day-to-day living through programs in family life education.

Basically, family life education is a service of planned intervention that applies the dynamic process of group learning to improving the quality of individual and family living. The manuals are in workshop format and offer possible new approaches of service to families. They are meant to serve as a training mechanism and basic framework for group leaders involved in FLE workshops.

In 1974, the Family Service Association of America appointed a National Task Force on Family Life Education, Development, and Enrichment. One of the goals of the Task Force was to assess the importance and future direction of family life education services within family service agencies. One of the recommendations of their report was to "recognize family life education, development, and enrichment as one of the three major services of the family service agency: family counseling, family life education, and family advocacy."[1] This recommendation was adopted by the Board of Directors of FSAA and has become basic policy of the Association.

An interest in family life education is a natural development of FSAA's role in the strengthening of family life and complementary to the more traditional remedial functions of family agencies. FLE programs can add a new dimension to the services provided by family agencies. They can open an agency to the general population by providing programs which are appropriate for all families and individuals, not only for those at risk. They provide a new arena for service that deals with growth as well as dysfunction. They can encourage agencies to look beyond the therapeutic approach and to take on a new objective for the enrichment and strengthening of family life. For the participants, FLE programs can lead to increased understanding of normal stress, growth of esteem for one's self and others, development of communications skills, improved ability to cope with problem situations, development of problem-solving skills, and maximization of family and individual potential.

---

1. "Overview of Findings of the FSAA Task Force on Family Life Education, Development, and Enrichment" (New York: Family Service Association of America, May 1976), p. 21 (mimeographed).

This series provides tangible evidence of FSAA's continuing interest in family life education and of a belief in its future importance for family services. FLE programs, coordinated within a total agency program and viewed as a vital and integral part of the agency, can become key factors in family service concern for growth and development within all families.

                                     W. Keith Daugherty

General Director

Family Service Association of America

TABLE OF CONTENTS

SESSION 5

INTRODUCTION TO THE MANUAL

The Family Life Enrichment program of Child and Family Services of Hartford, Connecticut, has developed a series of curricula relating to the specific stresses associated with the break-up and rebuilding of a family. Helping children deal with stress at a time when the adults may also be in stress is always a difficult task. This workshop, originally titled, "Effects of Divorce on Children," is designed to help parents respond to the unique effect their separation/divorce has had on their children, to recognize their own feelings within the process, and to strengthen the relationships between parent and child. Our objectives are to provide, through a supportive group experience, a means for parents: to be aware of their own and their child's feelings regarding the separation and to learn ways for both to express these feelings; to understand and support their own and their child's sense of self-worth; to help in re-enforcement of a clear communication style in the family, extended family, with friends and acquaintances; to evaluate and determine roles and responsibilities of the custodial and non-custodial parent in relation to the child.

In developing this workshop, it was our contention that the structure should clearly articulate overall objectives as well as objectives for each session. Goals include both the content to be learned and experienced as well as the development of process among group members. The content develops from the general (feelings about the separation) to the specific (custodial and noncustodial parents' relationships). The group process moves from situations of low risk in small subgroups to those dealing with more highly charged issues in a larger group. The curriculum is designed so that content in each session is presented in a way that anticipates the development of group process.

The process in each session includes the provision of information through mini-lectures and structured interaction among members in small subgroups, learning exercises that create a personal awareness of the issues being dealt with and help develop skills to deal with these issues, and discussion that will help to correlate information and personal skills and provide clarification.

Through experience with the workshop we have learned several things about its presentation. First, a thorough knowledge of the workshop as a whole--the objectives, content, and sequence--has been helpful to keep topic and questions in the perspective of the progression of

1

material. Second, group members will be reticent to risk their concerns early in the sessions, but, as the experience continues, they will be more likely to share. Thus, the curriculum calls initially for more leader involvement yet encourages members to participate through pairs. Third, because time is limited all of the concerns people bring to the group cannot be covered. By knowing what issues are introduced in the workshop and where, leaders can be clear with members on how and when the issues will be covered and can negotiate with the group about content left out. This knowledge is used to maintain content continuity, giving the leader clues about what discussion to encourage and what to hold off until later.

The workshop is designed to produce an equal balance among facts, feelings, and experiences. In this sense, the learning process is structured. Material is provided in a variety of ways throughout the curriculum to recognize that people learn in different ways at different times. Although the experiencing of feelings is encouraged, we distinguish between the therapeutic use of feelings as part of learning and the provision of a therapy service. We do not invite the ventilation of feelings, but rather a direct channeling of aroused feeling into a skill-building process. As group members are made aware of how they are feeling about significant issues, the task of the group changes to focus on the nature of decisions to be made to best use these feelings as motivators for action. Skills are taught which will help group members accomplish what they have decided.

This workshop works best with ten to fifteen participants. This provides for enough interchange without crowding. It works best with a heterogeneous group of men and women, custodial and noncustodial parents, of various ages. Both members of a separated/divorced couple have not been included in the same group, as we have felt that their leftover dissension would interfere with the group process.

Although we have developed a structured curriculum, we realize that each group and each group leader is different and, as such, the curriculum must be seen as a <u>guide</u> to directing learning rather than as an absolute. Thus, changes should be made in the basic curriculum to meet the style of the leader and the needs of the group.

2

GENERAL INFORMATION
ABOUT THE WORKSHOP

LENGTH: There are five sessions to be held in this workshop. Each session requires approximately two hours.

MATERIALS: All of the materials used in the workshop are relatively inexpensive and readily available. Most sessions require:

    flipchart or blackboard
    feltmarkers or chalk
    note pads
    pens or pencils
    note cards (3" X 5" and 5" X 8")
    copies of the handouts for each session

OPENING THE SESSION: At the beginnong of each session, bring up any issues that had to be left and finish this old business before starting on a new subject area. You may ask participants if they have any issues, questions, or concerns from the last session that they would like to discuss before you start the new session.

BRIEF OUTLINES: To inform participants of each session's material, put the Brief Outline for each session on a flipchart or blackboard and go over it briefly at the beginning of each session. It lets the group know what is to be covered that day.

MINI-LECTURES: The manual provides the basic information for each lecture. Present the mini-lecture in your own words, modifying it to suit your style and your group. You will want to assess the group's learning needs, expectations, and past learning experiences and then adapt this suggested content according to your judgment. A simple and informal way to present the material is to list key ideas on a flipchart, blackboard, or cards large enough for people to read. The flipchart also serves as a guide for your talk. Groups tend to respond more positively when the mini-lectures include such visual aids.

HOME ASSIGNMENTS: Some sessions require some work to be done out-side. The leader should go over the assignment and emphasize that it will be discussed at the following session. Encourage the group to complete the assignment, but do not place pressure on the participants to do so.

SESSION 1

SESSION 1

BRIEF OUTLINE

OBJECTIVES: To explore the feelings of both parent and child in relation to the divorce.

To help group members become more aware of their own feelings and those of their children as they relate to divorce.

To help members be aware that the feelings they are experiencing are shared and part of the process that most people in a similar situation experience.

To help members sort out their feelings and recognize that there are different ways people express their feelings.

To assist parents in helping their children sort out their feelings and to help them recognize the different ways children express feelings.

I. INTRODUCTION - GET ACQUAINTED

A. Participants fill out identification cards
B. Leader introduces self
C. Introduction of members
D. Purpose of workshop
E. Overview of format and content

II. FOCUSING ON THE COMMONALITY OF THE GROUP

A. Exercise One - Sharing Information
B. Exercise Two - Expressing Group Expectations

III. FEELINGS RELATED TO DIVORCE

A. Objectives
B. Mini-lecture
C. Exercises

IV. EXPRESSING FEELINGS
   A. Mini-lecture
   B. Discussion

V. SUMMARY

VI. HOME ASSIGNMENT

   HANDOUTS

SESSION 1

I. INTRODUCTION - GET ACQUAINTED

A. Fill Out Identification Cards

As members arrive, ask each to fill out an identification card. Ask members to include name, address, phone number, names and ages of their children, and if children are living at home or with the other parent.

The purpose of this exercise is to gather information about members which would be helpful to the group leader. The leader's knowledge of the names of members facilitates an informal and trusting group environment.

Have participants complete questionnaire (see page 23).

B. Leader Introduces Self

Once all group members have arrived, the leader introduces self, giving name, position or title, and any other appropriate identifying information. The leader may wish to share some personal information, such as marital status, ages of children, or professional background, that would facilitate empathy with the group.

C. Introduction of Members

The leader then asks members to introduce themselves to the group. Have participants give names and any other information they want to share, for example, are they now in the process of divorce or how long they have been divorced, number of children, age of children, and so on.

D. Purpose of the Workshop

It is necessary to define for the group the goals and purpose of family life education. It is also necessary to define the objectives of this group for parents who are in the process of divorce, or who are already divorced, as expressed by the sponsoring agency or organization.

It is essential to the members that the leader be supportive, clear, and understanding of their needs. The leader must help them learn to separate their role as parent from their role as spouse and deal with guilty feelings about depriving their children of the traditional two-parent "nuclear" experience.

"You are here because you are all parents who are divorced or in the process of a divorce. You are very concerned about how your children are affected by your divorce and how you can help them deal with themselves and with you in relation to the issues of the divorce.

"Parenting is a difficult and challenging task. The divorce process is difficult and also challenging because you are learning about and adjusting to a new family life-style. In this group, we will help you enrich the relationship you have with your child, help you to develop and enhance your role as an individual and as a parent. You are here because you care about your child, because you care about your relationship with your child."

E. Overview of Format and Content
   1. Describe group format
      "We will be using mini-lectures to provide you with information; experiental exercises in which you will actively work with ideas, concerns, and problems; and open discussions to bring mini-lectures, exercises, and personal concerns together."
   2. Overview of the workshop
      Distribute the course outline (see handout on pages 24 and 25)

II. FOCUSING ON THE COMMONALITY OF THE GROUP

"It is scary to jump right in and talk about one's children with people you do not know. Everyone here is concerned about and cares for their children. All of us are parents and are con-cerned about the effects of divorce on the children, caretaking, visitation, and parenting. These feelings are common to all members of the group--the fears and expectations, the questions, and the concerns.

"You will be listening, you will be looking, you will be think-ing, you will be working in this group. You will learn how to best use your own resources and the resources of those around you in dealing with these feelings."

10

A. Exercise I: Sharing Information
   1. Objective: To provide members with an opportunity to
      get acquainted with each other.
   2. Ask each participant to choose a partner and tell them
      one special thing about each of their children.
      Partner listens without commenting. After three
      minutes, members will switch roles so the other person
      can share the same type of information.
   3. Discussion: After members have been given time to share
      information about their child or children, ask the
      group to express their feelings about sharing this
      information. You may expect such comments as: "It
      is helpful to hear another person is worried about
      things I worry about." "I don't care to do much talking
      now. I'll wait until later." "I would like to hear
      what others have to say first."

      If members felt comfortable, develop how support and
      commonness is appropriate to members of this type of
      group.

You may want to go over the following points with the group:

"Some group members may be ready and comfortable to share
information about their children. At times, there are those
who are not ready and do not feel comfortable about sharing
information and the group must accept this. There are times
when people need space and time before they can speak in
the group situation.

"The group is responsible for itself and members are
responsible for themselves within the group. There are
times when people need space and time before they can
speak in the group situation.

"In summary, these are our goals for the next five sessions:

"To develop a more meaningful relationship with your children as you increase your awareness and understanding of
the variety of feelings experienced by parents and children
during the divorce process which are part of a normal
process of separation.

"To increase the awareness and clarity of the feelings and
language used by parents and children as they deal with

11

their feelings, using choices in developing a better sense of control over oneself.

"Strengths and skills developed by parents teach the child and provide children with optional tools they might use in dealing with their own feelings and experiences; parents act as models for their children."

B. Exercise 2: Expressing Group Expectations
1. Objectives: To provide group support and to stress the commonality of the group members; to help members realize that their objectives for attending the workshop are shared by others; and to let members know that their feelings are part of a "normal" separation process.
2. Exercise: Ask participants to choose a partner and to inquire what the partner's expectations are in coming to the group; they then reverse roles and the partner does the interviewing. "What do you hope to get out of coming to this group? What are your expectations in coming to this group?"

   Allow about three minutes for each partner to speak. Be aware of group process in this exercise. Some members will have difficulty in sharing the reasons that they are in the group. Some members will be quite anxious about their participation. It is important for the leader to assess each member and ascertain what techniques would be helpful to create a balance in the group process and help members participate.

   Some members may lose the focus of the exercise and begin talking about their own situations. You may have to remind them of the focus of the exercise:

   "Try to discuss with your partner what brought you to this group. I know you may want to share your personal situation with your partner and there will be an opportunity to do this in a later session. Please limit your discussion to what brought you to this group and what you hope to gain."
3. Discussion: When the time is up have members reform the larger group. (If the pair discussions are very

active, you may want to allow a few extra minutes before reforming the group.)

When the group is reformed, ask members to share openly with the group what they came up with in talking to their partners. Ask members to verbalize to the group their reasons for coming. Write these responses on a flipchart or blackboard.

As you hear responses from members, reflect the information back to the members and to the group-- tying in one response to another. Reflection is important. Relating the responses to one another, particularly while you are making personal assessments of members, helps to focus responses.

Examples: "I came because I am afraid of what is going to happen to me and to my children now that the divorce is final.

"I don't know if I can handle all the responsibility of the children and the house and my job.

"I don't know what to do about my anger toward my ex-spouse and I know it is really getting in the way when I try to deal with my child.

"I know my wife is setting me up so that my children will hate me and I don't know what to do about my kids. I still love my kids.

"I don't want to say anything; just listen."

Ask group if any of the responses are unique to any one person. Are the responses common to members of the group?

III. FEELINGS RELATED TO THE DIVORCE

A. Objectives
To help members become more aware of their own feelings and those of their children as they relate to divorce.

To help members be aware that the feelings they are experiencing are shared and a part of a "normal" process.

To help parents help their children express their feelings more easily.

B. Mini-Lecture
"There is a progression of feelings one experiences during separation and divorce that continues throughout the process and may continue for some time afterward. People experience a variety of feelings. You may not experience all of these feelings; you may experience them in varying order; and you may experience some more than once, at different times.

"During the crisis of separation and divorce, you go through a progression of stages. For example: The initial stage may bring intense feelings of denial, rage, anger, or blame. The transitional stage may bring feelings of frustration, hostility, bitterness, and resentment. The final stage may foster feelings of jealousy, doubt, loneliness, failure, and acceptance. Through the entire process some feelings may occur over and over: feelings of ambivalence, resentment, and the need to relive the situation to discover what happened.

"The stages may be experienced differently, and the feelings may be experienced differently. There is no right way to cope with the feelings involved in the divorce process. People are different and experience a variety of feelings. People change, feelings change-- day to day and month to month. It may take months, or even years to reach the stage of complete acceptance of one's self as a free and independent individual. The marriage becomes a part of one's past and a part of one's life experiences.

"Here are some examples of feelings you may experience:
self-blame	resentment	happiness +
guilt	acceptance +	failure
frustration	sadness	rejection
ambivalence	fear	annoyance
anger	panic	jealousy
hostility	relief +	doubts
bitterness	anxiety	loneliness."

14

C. Exercises
    1. Expressing feelings
        a. Objective: To help participants identify the
            feelings they are experiencing in relation to
            the divorce.
        b. Exercise: "Choose a partner and take three
            minutes to describe to your partner the feelings
            you are experiencing at this particular time of
            your life. Try to get in touch with the way you
            are feeling. Switch roles after three minutes,
            and remember to focus on feelings, not on
            situations."
        c. Discussion
            1. Ask members to share their feelings or those of
                their partners. List these feelings on the
                blackboard or flipchart. Place emphasis on
                feelings currently expressed. Members are
                usually at different stages of the separation
                process and thus a range of feelings will be
                expressed.
            2. Ask members to be aware of what it was like
                for them to express to their partner the feel-
                ings they are experiencing. This is an issue
                that will be discussed and developed later in
                the sessions. It is important for you to be
                supportive to members as they share with the
                group during this exercise.
    2. Feelings of Children
        a. Objective: To help parents identify the feelings
            their children may be experiencing during this
            stressful time.
            1. "Stay in the same pairs.
            2. "Describe to your partner how you think your
                children may be feeling in relation to your
                divorce. This may be difficult. It may help
                if you relate to how you are feeling. Are
                your children experiencing the same feelings?

                "What are some of the feelings your child may
                be experiencing? Have you noticed anything
                different in the way your child looks, is
                acting or what he is like day to day?
                    "My daughter is mad at me. She thinks it's
                    all my fault.
                    "My son doesn't want to help with any chores

now that his father is gone. He feels freer.

"Are your children's feelings the same or different from yours? Your child may be feeling
sad, lonely, angry, blameful, the same as you
do, but they are experiencing and expressing
in ways different from the way you do.

"How are the feelings the same?

"Your child may feel loss, loss of family, loss
of absent parent, status, money, security,
which may be the same as yours or different.

"Does how you are feeling affect how your
child feels?
   When you are sad your child may recognize
   your sadness. It might help him to know
   you are sad. 'I am feeling sad today and it
   helps that you understand and care.'

"Do you think your child feels things you may
not?

"Your child may feel he has no control over the
future and what happens to him. You know you
have control over what ultimately happens and
that you will not leave him.

"Your child may be angry at you.

"Children also experience loss in the divorce
process. They will go through stages of loss.
Children may feel different from their parents.
For example, sadness may be the same or may be
different. They may relate to their sadness
in different ways.

"There are times in a child's natural development when the separation of his mother and
father may affect him more intensely than at
other times."

Help parents recognize the importance of being aware of
their children's feelings.

Help them be aware that feelings may be the same or
different.

Help them be aware of how these feelings may be
different.

How we respond to feelings may be different, although
feelings themselves are the same. Use group as
example.

Use information shared in Exercise #2 to teach this.

IV. EXPRESSING FEELINGS

A. Mini-Lecture
"It is often difficult for us as adults to express our
feelings. We live in a society in which we are expected
to suppress our feelings. If it is difficult for us to
express our feelings regarding a very stressful situation,
imagine what children of any age must experience when they
don't know what to do with their feelings, particularly
when they do not understand them. Parents' feelings are
often mirrored in those of their children. Sometimes we
don't express our feelings at all. At other times, we
might express them in a negative fashion, taking it out
on the children. Neither of these approaches is healthy
or helpful.

"Some feelings are expressed in a negative way:

You may deprive or punish your child for no reasonable
cause simply to express your own feelings of self-
pitying anger.

You may yield to wishes indiscriminately because you
feel indifferent toward the child, or guilty because
of the current situation.

You may resent the child's presence; this is especially
true for a custodial parent. This may carry back to
the fact that pregnancy was not planned, or planned
in hopes of strengthening the marriage.

Annoyance at the ex-spouse for favors given to the child may be held against the child when he/she returns home.

"Whatever the feelings, whether you are experiencing them yourself, or feelings towards ex-spouse, or feelings you are transmitting to your children, IT IS IMPORTANT TO RECOGNIZE THEM AND SET THEM ASIDE TEMPORARILY SO THAT YOU HAVE MORE ENERGY TO GIVE TO YOUR CHILDREN AND CAN TAKE TIME TO HELP THEM EXPRESS THEIR FEELINGS.

"Children have many feelings about their parents' separation or divorce. Quite often they are afraid to express their feelings or do not know how to. It is important that you help your children express themselves.

"Why are children unable to express their feelings?

"Children learn from their parents. More often than not, parents may not express a lot of their feelings in front of their children, especially verbally. If children have not heard their parents express their sadness, grief, or joy, they do not know how to do it for themselves. You can help them by letting them know how you feel openly and honestly. This, however, should be done with discretion; feelings are difficult to express. We have never been taught how. We have often been taught to repress feelings. It can be frightening to express negative feelings.

"When something is wrong at home and children are not sure what is happening, they think the worst. If they don't verbalize their fears, then they feel that whatever is wrong won't come true, may it will go away.

"Parents can provide examples of expressing feelings in an open/honest way by saying:

'I'm feeling sad today.
'It hurts me that I can't give you the things that Daddy can.
'I'm feeling good today, we've all got each other.
'Of course I wish we were all together again, but mother and daddy just couldn't get along anymore.'

"Children often have feelings which they have difficulty expressing. They may just think these feelings without being able to express them verbally:

Sometimes I feel really scared; I worry about who's going to keep me safe. . . . Sometimes I feel so mad that I scream and cry (nonverbal way of expressing feelings). . . . Sometimes I feel sad and cry. I say I want to be alone but I really need people to help me. . . . Sometimes I think the divorce is my fault, I'm afraid the reason Mommy and Daddy were unhappy is because I was bad. . . . Sometimes I think I can make Mommy and Daddy get back together and be happy again if only I can be good enough. . . . Sometimes I pretend it never happened. . . . Sometimes I feel I have to be big and act more grown up. But I don't feel big. I'm still a little kid. . . . A divorce is really a confusing thing.[1]

"A child's responses or behavior may indicate how they are feeling (kicking, screaming, crying, hiding).

"Children need help in expressing themselves and need to feel that their parent is listening to them. Children express themselves verbally and nonverbally, therefore, parents have to be aware of all the messages their children are sending out. Parents can let children know they understand the feelings they are experiencing by mirroring back those feelings in a nonquestioning, nonjudgmental way. It indicates the parent's acceptance of those feelings and does not force the child to respond. Often, children find it difficult to admit they have these feelings. A reflective listening technique gives the child permission to have these feelings, whether he verbalizes them or not. For example:

"You must resent that mother (dad, I) broke up our home.

"It sounds to me that you miss dad tonight.

---

1. Janet Sinberg, <u>Divorce Is A Grown Up Problem</u> (New York: Avon, 1978).

"I am sure you blame me for not being able to go to camp this summer.

"It sounds to me that there are times you wish you could live on your own and not have to make a choice between dad and me."

B. Discussion
Review the list of feelings common to parents in the separation/divorce process (see page 14).

"You have listened to me talk about parents' feelings and about children and expressing their feelings. What are you feeling right now?"

Ask for comments from the group, using the reflective technique relating it to the board material, and tying member responses together. Here you are acting as a model for reflective style. Allow about ten minutes for group discussion on how parents express feelings and what skills they need to help their children.

V. SUMMARY

"In this session we have discussed our feelings in relation to the divorce and your children. We have talked about expressing our feelings, what feelings are common, and what we do with our feelings. Next week we will discuss listening and responding styles in communicating with children as well as with other adults."

VI. HOME ASSIGNMENT

"This assignment is designed to help you identify feelings you have had since your separation or divorce. You will learn that you have skills which have helped you cope better in certain situations."

HANDOUTS
FOR
SESSION 1

DIVORCED PARENTS

QUESTIONNAIRE #1

The following list represents possible areas of discussion in the workshop. Please indicate how helpful you feel each of these topics will be to you by checking the appropriate column next to each statement. Feel free to list additional suggestions.

		Very Little	Some	A Great Deal
A.	Better understanding of your children's feelings about the divorce.			
B.	Focus on how your child feels about both the custodial and non-custodial parent.			
C.	Increased understanding of how your child feels about himself.			
D.	Better understanding of how you feel about your children and your divorce.			
E.	Helping your child adjust to the role of being a "child of divorce."			
F.	Increased awareness of how divorce affects parent-child relationships.			
G.	Focus on the divorce triangle: child, custodial parent, non-custodial parent.			
H.				

OBJECTIVES OF WORKSHOP

Session 1:

To explore the feelings of both parent and child in relation to the divorce.

To help group members become more aware of their own feelings and those of their children as they relate to divorce.

To help members be aware that the feelings they are experiencing are shared and part of the process that most people in a similar situation experience.

To help members sort out their feelings and recognize that there are different ways people express their feelings.

To assist parents in helping their children sort out their feelings and to help them recognize the different ways children express feelings.

Session 2:

To create an awareness of how we listen, respond, and observe.

To teach skills to foster open, honest communication between parents and children.

To increase parents' listening skills.

To help parents communicate feelings.

To stress commonality of feelings of parents and children in divorce.

To be aware of nonverbal communication.

To increase parents' awareness of messages from children and what feelings are involved.

Session 3:

To strengthen and reinforce a positive self-image for parents and children.

To discuss the effects of high and low self-esteem.

To discuss the importance of self-esteem in building healthy parent-child relationships.

To discuss the factors necessary for building a child's self-image.

Session 4:

To identify the changing roles, responsibilities, and needs of parents in a divorce situation and how these changes affect the relationship between parents and children.

To teach the variety of reactions children may have to their parents' changing situation.

To identify specific concerns that affect the parent-child relationship.

To review the skills of observing and listening, and how these skills can be used.

To explore how parents' feelings affect their reactions to their children.

Session 5:

To identify specific concerns that occur in the divorce triangle between children and both parents; define how these concerns affect the children and define alternatives for dealing with these concerns in order to strengthen family relationships.

To help parents become aware of the importance of gender identity for children and identify how others can be helpful as role models.

To illustrate the effect of parents' dating behavior on their children.

To evaluate and summarize the workshop.

1. Make a list of some of the strong feelings you have had since your separation.

2. Make a list of five ways (good or bad) you have handled your feelings.

   (Think carefully about what you have done with your feelings. Your behavior as you were experiencing your feelings was an expression of your feelings.)

3. As you reflect upon ways you dealt with your feelings, you will learn certain things about the way you deal with your feelings. Some of the ways you have coped with them will be more productive than other ways. Each of us has handled our feelings better than at other times - at one time or another.

   Try to write down things you learned about yourself as you reflect back on those times.

   I learned that I have felt

   I did not like it when I felt

   I was glad when I

   I was surprised at myself when I

   I would like to

   I need to think about

   I can choose to

CHILDREN'S REACTIONS

A. How Might a Child React to Divorce?

Be prepared for a strong reaction.
1. Expression of grief.
2. May reject reality of parents separating (use of fantasy in play-of "Daddy coming back").
3. Has many questions disturbing him--many he is afraid to ask.
   What is going to happen?
   Who is going to look after me?
4. Fears of being isolated.

B. Feelings Child Might Experience in Relationship to Divorce:

Guilt: I did something to cause Mother and Daddy to separate.
Fear of Future: What is going to happen to me?
Fear of Rejection: Daddy left--is Mother going to leave me?
Resentment: Why did Mother and Daddy do this to me?
Hostility: Mother, you are to blame for Daddy leaving.
Shock: Can't believe parents are really separating.
Feelings of Abandonment: Can carry over to future--fear of abandonment.
Self-Pity: Why should this happen to me?
Rage: At parents or at self.
Frustration: Have no control over what is happening.

C. How do Children Express Selves Nonverbally?
A Child's Behavior Often Tells Us How He Is Feeling

Refusing to Eat: Expresses hostility.
Depriving Self: of food, pleasure, play.
Poor Sleep Habits
Doing Poorly in School
Playing Out Fantasies in story telling or games.
Bed Wetting
Acting Out: Unusual behavior at home or school (may be in only one place).
Quiet: when normally outgoing--or excessively noisy.
Any Behavior Which Differs from that previously experienced.

SESSION 2

SESSION 2

SESSION 2

BRIEF OUTLINE

OBJECTIVES: To create an awareness of how we listen, respond, and observe.
To teach skills to foster open, honest communication between parents and children.
To increase parents' listening skills.
To help parents communicate feelings.
To stress commonality of feelings of parents and children in divorce.
To be aware of nonverbal communication.
To increase parents' awareness of messages from children and what feelings are involved.

I. OPENING THE SESSION

A. Open Discussion
B. Review of Session I and Home Practice Exercise
C. Overview of Session

II. EXPRESSING FEELINGS

A. Exercise I: Listening Skills
B. Mini-lecture: Checking Out Messages
C. Exercise 2: Children's Messages and Feelings

III. MINI-LECTURE--SETTING LIMITS

IV. HOME ASSIGNMENT

HANDOUTS

SESSION 2

I. OPENING THE SESSION

A. Open Discussion
Generally you can expect a slight delay to allow time for
late arrivals. This time can be used for informal discussion
or issues left over from a previous session. Begin the
regular session as soon as possible.

B. Review of Session I and Home Practice Exercises
1. Briefly review material from last week's session.
Review material on feelings common to parents during
the separation/divorce process and feelings common to
children. Review expression of feelings covered during
first session.

"During the week, you were asked to be very aware of
strong feelings you have had during the divorce process
that you experienced and you thought about ways you
dealt with these feelings. Our feelings are communicated
to others. When we feel anger, we communicate our anger
and others (and often those closest to us) observe our
anger. Others also listen to our anger.

"When we feel happy, this feeling is communicated to
others. They see our happiness, they hear our
happiness."

Demonstrate this by using body language and verbal
language to communicate feeling. Role playing with
group gives permission and comfort to the group.
2. Refer to the handout assignment and ask the group to
think about looking and listening. Comment on learned
behavior we are often unaware of. Encourage feedback
regarding home exercises.

C. Overview of Session 2
Briefly go over what will be covered in session.

II. EXPRESSING FEELINGS

A. Exercise I: Listening Skills
1. <u>Objective:</u> To increase awareness of one's own listening skills.
2. Break the group into pairs.

   "Share with your partner a situation that occurred between you and your children in which you became very aware of the way that you listen and the way that you respond to them."
3. Partners in pairs will exchange roles, each taking a turn to share a listening and responding experience, being very aware of each other during the process.

   Allow 10-15 minutes for this exercise. Help pairs as necessary if they are losing their focus or get stuck with objectives.
4. <u>Discussion</u> Reform larger group and ask members to share their experiences with the group.

   "Without getting into details, what did you hear from your partner? Content is not the focus. Check out with your partner: Is it okay to share with the group? Look at partner and ask him/her about what you heard.

   "What was it like to listen?

   "What were you feeling as you were listening?

   "What do you think he/she was feeling?

   "Were you aware of your partner's face--his or her expression?

   "Were you aware of your own facial expression?

   "Were you aware of your partner's body?

   "Were you aware of your own body position as you were talking to each other?"

B. Mini-lecture--Checking out Messages
    "What we communicate to others are not only the verbal
    messages, but we are also communicating our feelings, our
    moods, our pleasures and displeasures, and our willingness
    to speak out or not to speak out. We use our entire person
    to communicate messages, and as we are doing so, the
    receiver--the person who is listening--is also sending
    messages about what he is hearing, what he is feeling, and
    messages about his entire person.

    "Checking out messages with one another is often overlooked.
    We assume a person meant one thing and we build our
    communications mostly on the way we hear and perceive the
    other person's messages. Checking out responses is asking
    the other person what he or she means and reflecting what
    we think back to the person.

        "Do you mean you. . . .

        "Are you feeling that. . . .

        "I am not clear on what you are saying about. . . .

    "Think about communication with your children. Last week we
    discussed what children may say as an expression of their
    feelings about the divorce. Often, true feelings may be
    masked and confusing. Sometimes we give confusing messages
    about what we say and how we look. For example, being angry,
    but talking in a very calm, soft, apathetic voice.

    "A twelve-year-old handicapped child with a hearing loss
    has withdrawn since the father left. The mother is feeling
    very guilty and sad, as evidenced by her body language.
    She is also bitter at her husband because she is left with
    the responsibility of reaching out to her son to help him
    deal with his loss.

    "A father affectionately speaks about his special seven-year-
    old daughter who will not speak to him. He blames his
    wife, is angry at her. His daughter ignores him when he
    picks up the other children; there is little eye contact but
    he feels she is telling him something and does not know how
    to respond.

"There are many other examples of what children may say and think about how these messages may be expressed. Think of what you may see and what you may hear.

"Just let Daddy come back, that's all. Don't send him away again.

"Why can't you both be together like before. You're mean not to let him come here.

"I don't want you to come here anymore--I don't like you and I hate you.

"I hate my school. I want to go away. I hate those kids. I hate you.

"If I wasn't so bad, maybe you would still be together.

"But what if . . . happens and. . . .

Or there is silence, a sad expression, and little eye contact.

"We have talked about the feelings related to divorce and there are many feelings represented in these statements. We will talk more about what children may experience in Session 4. Let us focus now on skills to deal with expressing feelings."

C. Exercise 2: Children's Messages and Feelings
    1. Objective: To increase parents' awareness of messages from children and what feelings are involved. To teach skills in communications with children, particularly around the stressful issues of divorce.
    2. Break into groups of three. (Option for leader: Do exercise as an open group.)
    3. "We have identified some of the feelings related to divorce. Think now of a situation in which you sense your children felt a certain way: happy, sad, angry, lonely, rejected." Allow 3 minutes.
    4. Discussion. Use the following questions to encourage discussion.
            How did they express their feelings?
            What did you observe? How did they look?

36

What did your children say?
What were their feelings? Did you check them out
with them?
What were your feelings?
What did you say to them?
How did they respond?
How did you feel about their responses?
How could you have handled the same situation using
a different listening technique?
Would you have felt better?
Have you ever used a different technique as you were
listening to your children?
What was your body doing?
Were you touching your child?
Were you looking directly at him?

"For example: Boy: 'Ever since Dad left, I have to do
all the work around here. It's all
your fault.'

Face downcast, no eye contact, slams door.
What is he feeling?

Mother: Responded angrily at child,
yelling unreasonably at her own
anger, not at child's anger.
Mother may be feeling guilt,
hurt, blame, and anger which may
be misdirected.

"Sometimes our own feelings about a situation get in the
way of honestly and openly dealing with what the other
person is expressing to us. If we are feeling angry
about the divorce, we may respond to our own feelings of
anger as a child is saying, 'Just let Daddy come back--
that's all. Don't send him away again.'

"On the other hand, if we are feeling good about a new or
fresh situation--getting a job, moving to a new neighbor-
hood--we may not fully appreciate a child's apprehensions
or fears about the situation and may respond to our own
good feelings, saying, 'Everything is fine, dear; you
will get used to it.'

"Children look at things differently than adults.
Children may react differently to certain things.

"We have discussed observing, listening and reflecting
what you see and hear as a way of letting your children
know you understand and respect their feelings. It also
gives them permission to express their feelings verbally,
knowing that they will be accepted by you in a nonjudgmental way. This means you will respond to your
children without being judgmental. Accept their feelings
and let them know that you are accepting them.

"There may be times when you do not have the emotional
or physical energy to do this. Letting your children
know that you need time for yourself is giving yourself
permission for time that you need and also providing
them with permission to let others know when they feel
they need time. At times, this will be time away from
you.

"As children recognize that they have permission to
express themselves or may choose to take time away for
themselves, they will begin to feel more free to express
themselves openly and honestly. This is the first step
in helping a child begin to communicate more openly
with you."

Invite members to comment and share experiences. Focus
discussion on the different reactions from adults and
from children.

III. MINI-LECTURE: SETTING LIMITS

"Parents have a responsibility to set limits and provide
consistency within the home. For the single parent, this can
be more difficult to maintain. However, now more than ever it
is essential to provide limit-setting and a consistent atmosphere, particularly since the separation process evokes many
insecure and isolated feelings in children. Often, guilt over
the separation leads the single parent to overlook limits to
appease personal guilt. This can only add to the confusion and
apprehension of the children.

"Communicating openly, firmly, and honestly is crucial to the consistent atmosphere so necessary during the separation and divorce process. Reasonable limits and open communications will encourage a trusting, caring environment.

"The parent should indicate appreciation to the child whenever possible to promote feelings of self-worth:

'I understand the chores may be frustrating for you.'

'Each of us must do his work so that we can all enjoy time together.'

'I do appreciate all the work you are doing to help at home.'

'It really pleases me to see you do your share.'

"Open communication and the freedom to express and share feelings sets the tone for building and enhancing the self-worth of both parent and child.

"All of us do things that help us feel good about ourselves. We can also choose to handle difficult situations in talking to our children and listening to our children. Learn from the past what has helped you to like yourself."

IV. HOME ASSIGNMENT

Distribute handout, "Growing and Learning About Oneself."

The handout is designed to help parents become aware of what they have done to re-enforce their strengths and resources.

Briefly go over the exercise to answer any questions group members may have.

HANDOUT
FOR
SESSION 2

GROWING AND LEARNING ABOUT ONESELF

Write down four things you <u>like</u> about yourself using a couple of words or a phrase. Think in terms of good feelings you have about yourself, or ways you react to a particular situation.

Example: I was able to accept my son's quiet, sad behavior and appreciate his need for space and time away from me without feeling he was rejecting me and not appreciative of what I was doing for him.

Next to these four feelings write down the opposite feelings. (This could be how you felt while growing up in your family before you began to feel good about these particular things.)

Example: I used to feel I was not appreciated and would angrily complain when my family did not seem to smile and appreciate all I did for them.

1.

2.

3.

4.

1.

2.

3.

4.

SESSION 3

SESSION 3

BRIEF OUTLINE

OBJECTIVES: To strengthen and re-inforce a positive self-image
for parents and children.
To discuss the effects of high and low self-esteem.
The importance of self-esteem in building healthy
parent-child relationships.
To discuss the factors necessary for building a
child's positive self-image.

I. OPENING THE SESSION

   A. Brief Review of Session 2
   B. Discuss Home Assignment
   C. Brief Overview of Session 3

II. MINI-LECTURE--SELF-WORTH

   A. Objective
   B. Children and Self-worth
   C. Parents and Self-worth

III. EXERCISES

   A. Defining High and Low Self-esteem
   B. Identifying with Your Children's Feelings

IV. BUILDING CHILDREN'S SELF-ESTEEM

   A. Mini-lecture
   B. Exercise

V. HOME ASSIGNMENT

HANDOUTS

SESSION 3

I. OPENING THE SESSION

A. Review of Session 2
If any issues are left unfinished at the last session, the leader should bring these up for discussion.

B. Discuss Home Assignment
Make reference to the home assignment regarding learning and growing. Ask group for any feedback. Encourage responses and focus on awareness of the growth process.

C. Brief Overview of Session 3
Using the Brief Outline, give a short overview of what will be happening in this session.

II. MINI-LECTURE: SELF-WORTH

A. Objective
To teach that the feelings group members have of themselves as parents and as people, particularly related to separation, have an impact about the way their children feel about themselves.

B. Children and Self-worth
"The single most important factor in forming your child's basic personality structure is his self-concept. A child's self-concept is the mental picture he has of himself. It is like a mental map. How a child behaves depends on the mental maps by which he is guided. Your child's most important mental map is his self-concept, what he thinks of himself. His success in school, in his community, now and in later life depends to a large extent upon his self-concept.

"His self-esteem is particularly important at the time of divorce in his family for he may feel very much alone and isolated in his world, as well as isolation from his teachers, classmates, and friends. This isolation derives from the feelings discussed in the first session and which arise again and again. These may be feelings the child does not understand, which make him feel badly and make him feel he is different from everybody else he knows.

"The child who feels good about himself is the one who gets along meeting his day-to-day experiences and handling them the best way he can. He is the one who learns the most, who can meet new people and situations with confidence. He is the one who can say, 'I am good. I am likeable. I can do things. I can try new things and be successful.'

"Then, there are children who do not feel very good about themselves; they are the ones who see themselves as 'I am not very good. I am not likeable. I cannot do things, especially new things. There is no sense in trying because I won't succeed anyway.' These are children who are problems to themselves and to others. These are the children who have the most difficulty learning, meeting new people, and trying new situations.

"Some people, children and adults alike, generally have a pretty good feeling about themselves while others continually feel low about themselves. That does not mean that the individual who feels good about himself doesn't have some days when he is 'down', but feeling 'down' is not a normal pattern in his life."

C. Parents and Self-worth
"The separation/divorce process is a stressful time in one's life. Your self-worth may easily be shaken as you experience the rejection, the feelings of failure, the ambivalence, the fear, the anger, and the guilt which occur as part of the normal process of separation and the dissolving of a marriage.

"When you, 'the parent', feel good about yourself, when your self-worth is high, you feel full, honest, responsible; you feel you love and can be loved, you feel you are worth something, you feel that because of you the world is a better place, you feel you can contribute to your own sense of being and to others.

"You can learn about yourself. You realize that although there are times when you may feel pretty low, you can begin again and handle the problems you must face. You care about yourself and you care about others.

"When you, 'the parent', feel low and don't feel good about yourself, you feel empty, you may feel dirty, you may feel guilt, shame, uselessness and that you are worth nothing. The world means nothing to you and you mean nothing to it. When you feel this way, when you recognize that you are feeling this way and want to do something about it, you are coping and then choosing what to do about it. When you choose to do something about yourself, for yourself, you are struggling to regain your self-worth and feel good again. Sometimes it may be necessary to seek help to do this. Sometimes you may be able to do this through your own resources.

"Yet all of us, adults, young adults or children, can work toward creating a full sense of self-worth for ourselves-- the 'I am somebody' feeling.

"The feeling of self-worth, the 'I am somebody' feeling, is particularly important for children affected by divorce. You, as a parent, have a responsibility to yourself and to your children to develop your sense of self-worth--and to feel that you are somebody, someone worth being listened to, being heard, being responded to, and owning your feelings."

III. EXERCISES

A. Defining High and Low Self-esteem
This exercise is done in two parts. In both parts, parents are asked to try to recall what it was like for them to experience feeling high and feeling low.

1. Ask members to break into groups of three.

"Share with your partners a recent moment when your spirits were up. For example:

"You were recognized at work for resolving a particularly difficult problem.

"You successfully handled a difficult situation with your child.

"You redecorated a room in your house at minimum cost, creating a fresh new look and a good feeling for you.

"You got through the first step in securing a job-counseling interview to help you define your skills.

"What was it like for you? Try to feel again the feelings you had that day."

Ask members to share their feelings and encourage their partners to reflect what each of them hears. Each person of the subgroup takes a turn sharing. Allow approximately 20 minutes.

2. Discussion
    Reassemble the larger group. List group responses on the flipchart or blackboard.

3. Use the same method to ask members to recall a recent situation when they were feeling low. Usually it is easier for group members to recall feeling low because they often think of themselves as being down over the separation and divorce experience.

    "Reform the same groups of three. I would like you to do the same exercise with a recent situation in which you were feeling low, even though it may be painful. For example,

        "You were reprimanded by your boss.

        "You were not invited to a traditional family gathering even though your children were.

        "Your child is verbally abusing you because your ex-spouse is not living at home."

4. Discussion
    Reform larger group. List members' responses, reflecting what members are saying. Encourage members to clarify their responses.

    Encourage discussion about what feelings are like when they feel high and when they feel low. Encourage group support and reflection. For example:

"No doubt, when you feel good about yourself,
you seem to be able to handle anything.

"If only you wouldn't let people get to you to
make you feel so helpless and so low. It's almost
like you can <u>not</u> let them do that to you if you
try hard enough.

"I wonder if my daughter can feel as low as that
and she isn't the one getting the divorce, I am.

"All of us become low at one time or another and all of
us go through highs. The point is that we want to feel
good about ourselves and that we do care about ourselves. How do we help children to feel good about
themselves?"

B. Identifying with Your Children's Feelings
   1. Objective: To help parents identify with the feelings
      of children.
   2. Exercise
      This exercise can be done in small groups or individ-
      ually. Assess the strength of the process and the
      discussions. An individual approach to this exercise
      may allow some space for members, particularly when
      discussion has been lengthy. Small groups may be
      appropriate when members are very supportive and are
      benefiting from the reflective styles of one another.

      If this exercise is done individually, provide pencils
      and note pads for group members. If this exercise is
      done in small groups, ask the group to form subgroups.

      "Think of a stressful situation when you were a child
      and something happened or somebody said something to
      you that made you feel bad. Remember how you felt
      during that incident, how you felt as a child. As you
      remember that time, how do you wish it could have
      happened? What would you have wished could have
      happened that would have helped you to feel better
      about yourself? Were you pleased about what did
      happen and how you felt about yourself? For example:

      "Your first experience of a racial or ethnic slur
      that you recognized that the slur referred to you.

Feelings of anger, flight, denial, and identification may have been experienced. You may have wished that something terrible would happen to the person saying those words, but soon you were probably looking for a parent to help understand what was said and why it caused the reaction it caused in you. Perhaps you were seeking comfort, or a sense of not being alone, or a way to understand what happened. Your sense of self-worth had been attacked, and you may have been looking for someone to restore your good feelings."

3. Allow several minutes for members to write down the incident or to discuss it in small groups.

4. Discussion
Reform larger group if the exercise was done in small groups. Ask group members to describe their experiences. Help them to focus on what they remember feeling. Relate their responses to feeling high or feeling low and refer back to flipchart or blackboard for feelings listed from the previous exercise. For example:

"I wanted time alone.

"I felt very afraid.

"I needed people to understand me.

"I felt so good that my parents were supportive even though they had every right to be angry with me.

"I wanted someone to listen to me even though I didn't know how to tell them so."

Emphasize that parents must try to identify with the feelings of their children to understand these feelings and to help the children deal with these feelings.

IV. BUILDING CHILDREN'S SELF-ESTEEM

A. Mini-lecture
"In the last session we talked about your children's feelings and how to help them express them. But children must feel good about themselves before they can express

their feelings--both positive and negative. Children
affected by divorce may have a difficult time feeling good
about themselves.

"They may feel they are to blame, that they are not
lovable, that they are in the way, that they are keeping
their mother and father from doing something else. Any of
the feelings discussed last week would affect a child's
self-esteem: anger, guilt, sadness, resentment, frustration, helplessness, relief.

"We also discussed feelings and helping children to express
them through reflective listening. This same technique
can be used to help children feel good about themselves.
We can also build children's self-esteem by the way we
reply to them, whatever it may be.

"What happens when children feel good about themselves?
They demonstrate integrity, honesty, responsibility,
compassion, love, a belief in themselves, are able to ask
for help, appreciate their own worth, and are ready to
see and respect the worth of others.

"What do our children need to feel good about themselves?
Three considerations necessary for self-esteem are:
emotional factors, supportive relationships, and competency
factors. These factors are necessary for all children but
have added implications for children affected by divorce."
1. Emotional Factors. Have group members give suggestions.
        For example:
            Love
            Self-importance
            Independence
            Uniqueness
            Physical comfort
            Security
            Continuity in relationships
            Trust
            Compassion
            Integrity
            Acceptance
            Honesty
            Self-esteem
2.   Relationships.
        a.   "All children need a positive system of

self-evaluation. This comes from self-reinforce-
ment as well as from other people, the significant
others in their lives. Self-esteem can become very
fragile when children feel that they have lost the
most significant people in their lives, their
parents. I refer to both parents, regardless of
who has custody, because children may feel they
have lost both, emotionally at least, because both
parents may be involved in their own problems.
This sense of loss pervades the entire divorce
process for children and can have a decided impact
on the self-esteem (loss of parents, security,
family unit, losing a sense of belonging, respect
from others, and so on).

"It is important that the children continue to have
close contact with significant others in their
environment. We all serve as models by what we say
and do and that leads to reinforcement.

"Significant others include: custodial parent,
absent parent (noncustodial), grandparents (both
sides), extended family, teachers, schoolmates,
baby-sitters, playmates, boyfriends, girlfriends,
adult friends.

"One learns to appreciate one's own worth not only
from how one feels about oneself but also through
reinforcement from others. Generally, it is a
child's parents and teachers who have the most
impact in reinforcing self-regard, but, in times
of stress, children may need the significant others
in their lives to help to reinforce their self-
worth. These may be nonthreatening individuals,
not intimately involved in the stressful changes
occurring in the children's lives, who may serve
as role models."
    b.   Allow time for participants to discuss the roles
         that significant others play in children's lives,
         to help them develop and maintain a sense of self-
         worth. Focus on self-esteem, not on the signifi-
         cance of relationships.
  3. Competency Factors.
      "We have talked about the importance of emotional
      supports and those of significant others in helping

a child develop a positive sense of self-worth.
Although we recognize these as essential ingredients,
they may be too conceptual for children to hook into
at a time when everything may seem to be going wrong.

"This is why it is important to be aware of your
children's competency in a special area or areas and
to be able to use these as honest and open reinforcement for the child. We immediately think of special
talents and skills: academics, sports, music,
writing, and art. But what of the child who lacks a
special talent or skill?"

Have a brief open discussion of what competency
parents can focus on, no matter how small. Examples
to help parents: riding a bicycle, tossing a ball,
cooking a meal, dressing neatly, coordinating colors
well, neatness of school work, or consideration of
others.

"It is extremely important that parents (and significant others) be honest in their praise (rein-
forcements). Children recognize insincerity.

"We are discussing issues of parenting in general.
We are also discussing issues relating to divorce.
They may overlap; wise parenting will often carry
over into issues of divorce."

B. Exercise
    1. "Describe a situation relating to the divorce in which
        your children said or did something which evoked a
        response from you. Focus on a positive response, a
        negative response, or the behavior which accompanied
        the response. Consider the following questions as you
        think of the situation:
            Do you think your response made your child feel
            good or bad?
            How did you feel about your response?
            Could it have been changed to make your child
            feel better about himself?

        "For example,
            Child mows the lawn or some other big job tracks
            grass (dirt/mud) into the house.

Child comes home from school late but breathless
because he had stayed after to help the teacher,
at teacher's request.

Child is happy, exuberant, but has stereo turned
up too high.

Child comes home from visiting with other parent,
feeling very good because he has had a good time.
He may say, 'Why don't we go out to dinner like
Daddy and I do?'

Child comes home crying: 'Jimmy says I'm different because my mommy and daddy are divorced.'

Daughter comes home with invitation to father-
daughter banquet and her father does not live
nearby.

Father forgets to pick up children on weekend that
is supposed to be spent with him."
2. Break the group into small subgroups. Each subgroup
    member will take a turn and share an experience with
    the small group, partners should be encouraged to
    comment and support subgroup.
3. Reform larger group. Using the questions given at
    beginning of exercise have participants relate
    responses to factors needed for self-worth: emotional,
    relationships, and competency.

"How we treat our children often determines how they feel about
themselves. When something goes wrong, over which the children
have no control, the situation and their worthiness should be
separated. When things go well children should be helped to
feel that it is okay to feel good about themselves.

"How can we help our children feel good about themselves? As
parents we have a tremendous amount of influence over this.
It is just as easy to enhance the self-worth of children as
it is to put them down. We have the power to respond to all
children in negative ways, positive ways, and neutral ways.
It is up to us to decide which is most helpful to our children
and, consequently, makes us feel better.

"Let me conclude with this quote from Virginia Satir:

Every word, facial expression, gesture or action on the part of the parent gives the child some message about his worth. It is said that so many parents don't realize the effect these messages have on the child, and often don't even realize what messages they are sending. A mother may accept the bouquet clutched in her three year old's hand and say, "Where did you pick these?"--Her voice and smile implying "How sweet of you to bring me these. Where do such lovely flowers grow?" This message strengthens the child's feeling of self-worth. Or she might say "How pretty" but add, "did you pick these in Mrs. Randell's garden?"--implying that the child was bad to steal them.

This message would make him feel wicked and worthless. Or she might say, "How pretty! Where did you pick them?" but wear a worried, accusing expression that added, "Did you steal them from Mrs. Randell's garden?" In this case, she is building low self-esteem but probably does not realize it.[1]

V. HOME ASSIGNMENT

"Parents and Self-Image," and "Children and Self-Image."

The home assignment handouts are designed to encourage awareness of past experiences. It is useful to help parents define strengths, and to recognize these strengths as positive tools and then how to use them.

1. Virginia Satir, Peoplemaking (Palo Alto, Calif.: Science and Behavior Books, 1972), p. 25.

HANDOUTS
FOR
SESSION 3

PARENTS AND SELF-IMAGE

1. Write down a problem you may be having with your child.

2. Decide what you can do to resolve this problem--what will help.
   a. What are risks?
   b. What anxieties will it cause?
   c. Are they realistic?

What will encourage you to feel good about your own esteem?

What worked?

I felt

I felt badly when

I felt good when

I learned that

I will remember to

I need to

CHILDREN AND SELF-IMAGE

Write down an incident that helped you to feel good about your child.

What had you done that helped you to feel good?

What had your child done that helped you to feel good?

Do you think your child felt good? How do you know this?

How did you share this experience?

I learned that

I felt good when

I must remember to

I learned that

SESSION 4

SESSION 4

BRIEF OUTLINE

OBJECTIVES: To identify the changing roles, responsibilities, and needs of parents in a divorce situation and how these changes affect the relationship between parents and children.
To teach the variety of reactions children may have to their parents' changing situation.
To identify specific concerns that affect the parent-child relationship.
To review the skills of observing and listening, and how these skills can be used.
To explore how parents' feelings affect their reactions to their children.

I. OPENING THE SESSION

A. Open Discussion
B. Review Home Assignment
C. Brief Overview of Session

II. CHANGING ROLES AND NEEDS OF PARENTS

A. Mini-lecture
B. Exercise

III. HOW CHANGES AFFECT PARENT-CHILD RELATIONSHIP

A. Mini-lecture--Children's Behavior and Feelings
B. Exercise
C. Mini-lecture--Handling Conflictual Situations
D. Discussion
E. Exercise

IV. HOME ASSIGNMENT

HANDOUT

SESSION 4

I. OPENING THE SESSION

A. <u>Open Discussion</u>
Briefly discuss any leftover issues.

B. <u>Review Home Assignment from Session 3</u>
"Did any of you have an experience this week related to
building of self-worth in your child? Would you be
willing to share it briefly with group?"

C. <u>Brief Overview of Session</u>
Go over the Brief Outline for Session 4.

II. CHANGING ROLES AND NEEDS OF PARENTS

A. <u>Mini-lecture</u>
"Many things happen to the adults in a separation/divorce
situation, for both the custodial and noncustodial parent.
There are role changes, the custodial parent generally
has to assume additional responsibilities while giving up
others. The noncustodial parent traditionally gives up
many roles and those he or she retains have a different
connotation. As an example, the custodial parent may feel
he or she has to be a 'super parent', while the noncustodial parent becomes a part-time parent, and even that
role may not be very satisfactory. These roles may not
be satisfactory to the children either. Along with the
changing roles come needs for the parent--some new ones,
intensification of others, as well as feelings relating
specifically to these changes.

"We are going to take time to find out how you see your
roles having changed recently, whether your needs have
changed, and how you feel about these changes. Later on
we will relate these changes to how your child is reacting
and see whether or not these factors are creating conflict
in your relationship.

"For example, changing roles may change needs which in
turn affects feelings:

"Role of being single again creates needs for sexual satisfaction, affection, and closeness with an adult of the opposite sex. Such needs may result in feelings of frustration, longing, resentment for being in such a situation, and anxiety that needs may never be met.

"Role of being single again may create some needs as mentioned above, and when these needs are met there is feeling of love, warmth, feeling good about self which in turn may be transmitted to children.

"If father has custody, he must assume new duties such as housekeeping, food shopping, cooking, doing laundry, and providing for personal needs of children. He may feel overwhelmed and inadequate. Children's roles in this situation change because they may have to help with chores and they may resent these changes in their lives.

"The mother who takes on a job assumes major dual roles of mother and provider. As the single head of house she may feel overwhelmed, resentful, and guilty of not being able to concentrate fully in either role, be it mother or employee.

"The role of a single parent in social and school situations may create feelings of being different and wanting acceptance.

"The noncustodial mother struggles with the guilt of not fulfilling the traditional mother role or fulfillment of her own needs."

B. Exercise
1. Break group into subgroups of four.

Ask members to discuss the following question:

"How have your roles and responsibilities changed since your separation/divorce? Relate this specifically to responsibilities relating to your children." Allow time for each member to share with the small group. This is for both custodial and noncustodial parents.

"Examples: Sole disciplinarian
              Wage earner
              Responsible for all outside/inside
              housework
              Only adult in family/companion to children
              Multiple roles
              Loss of 'homemaker' role
              'Part-time parent', limited disciplinarian,
              provider but no say in how money is spent,
              seen as 'sugar daddy' or miser, artificial
              situation when with child
              Loss of husband/wife role
              Loss of 'complete family' status
              Loss of responsibilities in the home."

2. Discussion
    Ask members for the new roles and responsibilities they
    found themselves assuming and list them on the flip-
    chart or blackboard.

3. "What do you need for yourself in order to accomplish
    your new role or responsibilities? For example,
          Time, more time with children
          Money
          Space
          Adult Companionship
          Advice
          Sharing of Responsibility
          Affection."

4. Discussion
    Help members differentiate between those roles they
    must accept and those they have some choice in
    assuming. The following questions can be used to
    stimulate discussion:

    How do you feel about these changes? About your
    needs?

    Have these changes in roles been necessary or are you
    assuming a new role or additional ones in the role
    of martyr?

    What kinds of feelings do you experience in relation
    to these changes?

    Examples of feelings parents might be experiencing in
    relation to their changing roles and needs: resentment,

71

anger, tiredness, fear, being overwhelmed, loneliness, relief, anxiety, bitterness, feeling in control or out of control.

III. HOW CHANGES AFFECT PARENT-CHILD RELATIONSHIP

A. Mini-lecture--Children's Behavior and Feelings

"Children may react in many different ways to the changes occurring in their parents' lives. As we mentioned in the first session, children often do not know what labels to put on their feelings or what to do with them, particularly when they relate to something as unsettling as the divorce of their parents. Often, unsettled feelings become unsettled behavior. Let's look briefly again at some of the feelings, what they might indicate, and how they might be expressed by children.

1. "Anger: Children may be angry for a number of different reasons. They may be angry at the parent for 'letting/making Dad (Mom) leave', they may show anger because they feel guilty about the separation. Anger is expressed when one parent doesn't have enough time or energy to satisfy the child; the child resents this and is asking for more attention, direction, or firmness.

   "Children may demonstrate their anger or other feelings through a drop in school grades; acting out behavior at school, home, or in the community; or they may withdraw from family, teachers, or friends.

2. "Guilt: Children may feel they are responsible for all that has happened and may act out (bad behavior) to reinforce their feelings of 'I am bad--I am to blame for this situation.' Their guilt may also be conveyed through fearfulness and anxiety.

3. "Grief: Expressions of grief and sadness should not be repressed. Also, children may be unable to express their grief regarding the divorce; parents showing their grief may help children express their own grief.

4. "Rejection of Reality: Children may not admit that Daddy (Mommy) has really left and may use fantasy in play as part of the denial process. This is okay, they will eventually grow out of it.

5. "Resentment: Children may resent not having Mom (Dad) at home, may resent not having the extras previously enjoyed, or may just feel self-pity--why did this

happen to me? Children may react in many different ways--may play on their parent's sympathies, whine, or exhibit unusual behavior.

6. "Fear: Fear of what will happen to them, fear of someone replacing the absent parent, fear of rejection, fear of the future. Children may be afraid to ask questions: 'What is going to happen to me? Who is going to look after me?'

7. "Loss: Children may feel many losses in this separa- tion, just as parents do: loss of parent, loss of status as a 'complete' family. Connected with this is a sense of insecurity, therefore it is important to make as few changes regarding the children as possible, particularly in the initial stages of the separation/ divorce.

8. "Loneliness: Both parents and children are expe- riencing the loneliness associated with a loss and may crave attention. Children's best known means of getting attention is by unusual behavior. If they can't get 'good strokes' (attention for good behavior), they will do bad things and settle for 'bad strokes'.

9. "Other types of behavior that children may exhibit include: refusing to sleep; depriving self; poor sleep habits; fear of food, pleasure, or play; doing poorly in school; fighting, bullying, whining, or crying; being sullen, withdrawn, or excessively quiet or noisy; bed wetting; unusual behavior in either home or school (may or may not be both).

"What other reactions or types of feelings have you observed in your own children to add to this list?"

Limit time for this conversation, but give the group an opportunity to make additions. Do not allow them to get into issues, as this is part of the next exercise.

B. Exercise
1. Objective: To identify specific concerns of group members relating to their relationship with their children.
    Review skills used to deal with these concerns.
2. Break the group into subgroups of three or four.
    Ask members to discuss these questions, giving each member time to participate:

"What specific situations relating to your
separation/divorce have caused conflict between
you and your child?
"How do you deal with these conflicts?"
3. Reform larger group to discuss the following:
"Have the changes you have been discussing been
of concern to you?
"If so, in what way?
"How about your reactions or responses?"
4. Ask members to identify specific concerns which can be
listed on the flipchart or blackboard. The purpose of
this part of the exercise is to have members share
commonality in concerns relating to children.

C. Handling Conflictual Situations
"In Session 3 we discussed observing and listening to
your children. When tensions are high it may help to
slow down, to refrain from saying the first thing that
comes to mind. A useful thing to do is to observe what
is going on carefully. Is it actually as bad as you
thought originally, or have you read things that aren't
there into it? As we discussed earlier, listening is one
of the most important things one can do. As one listens
the speaker may be able to work through some of his/her
feelings without having to become defensive. The listener
can also cool down his/her own feelings relating to self
and his/her feelings relating to the children.

"Here are some helpful thoughts in dealing with stress and
improving relationships with the children:

"When feeling angry be sure your anger is expressed to
the person at whom it is directed. If you are angry
at your ex-spouse, don't find an excuse to get angry
at your children because your ex-spouse isn't around.

"Let your child know why you are angry; be open and
honest.

"Allow children to express their resentments.

"Children's expression of feelings by nonverbal
behavior should be acknowledged by their parent.

"Continue firmness and structure in your children's
lives even if it seems easier to be more relaxed.
You may never have had an opportunity before to stress
consistency with the children if you were always
concerned about problems with your spouse.

"Help the children have a sense of continuity with
both parents, even if it is painful to you.

"There is no need to feel guilty if you want a life
separate from the children. Plan time for yourself
apart from the children and with the children.

"Help alleviate the children's anxieties by not talking
of your own anxieties in front of them.

"Help the children express some feelings of sadness by
letting them see you express yours.

"Don't give false hopes of reuniting with the spouse.

"With some of these thoughts in mind let's get back to how
you handled the situations you discussed in your subgroups
and we listed on the board."

D. Discussion
    1. "Did you feel the way you handled the situation was
        effective or not? What specific communication skills
        did you use? What alternatives might you have tried?

        "Relate different ways of handling changed behavior to
        use of the communication skills previously discussed
        and practiced: listening, observing, reflective
        listening, and the methods discussed in the mini-
        lecture."
    2. Give members support in that the concerns they have
        are shared with others. Teach that there are skills
        they possess which can be used in dealing with situa-
        tion and therefore improving relationship with the
        children at this time.

        "You really can control what you do. You have the
        capacity to use these skills: listening, looking,
        caring, and reflecting what you see and hear, and
        sharing feelings. Also, you can separate your

feelings from those the child may be feeling; separate your child's feelings from the feelings related to the situation; respect his or her feelings; and accept his or her feelings."

E. Exercise
"Earlier we discussed the feelings children have in relation to their parents' separation/divorce and the behavior and reactions that express their feelings. We also discussed your feelings at this particular time. How you feel has direct relation to how you react with your children, whether you intend that to be the case or not."
1. Have participants reform their subgroups to discuss how the changed needs and feelings of previous exercises may be affecting their relationship with their children.

"For example: The need to be both mother and father to child, or a 'superparent.'
Anger when feeling frustrated, guilty, or overburdened.
Resentments taken out on child.
Need to alleviate guilt by being too easy.
Need for time for self when there isn't enough time for anything.
Anxiety for the future is passed on to child."

2. Discussion
Reform larger group to discuss:

"How have these feelings affected relationships with your children?

"Have they been reasonable reactions or blown out of proportion to the situation?" Refer back to ways of handling situations. Help members identify reasonable reactions versus unreasonable reactions to use as a guide in future encounters with children at stressful times. Present alternatives for dealing with these reactions.

Examples of reactions: Reasonable: Coming home tired from work and having the kids jump on you, so you yell for peace and quiet for a while.

Unreasonable: Kids playing game and you come into
room and yell at them for making too much noise
because you are feeling depressed.

Allow time for discussing alternative ways of dealing
with situations. Provide support for members and
reinforce actions which appear to work, using material
from the session for teaching purposes.

IV. HOME ASSIGNMENT

The chart (see page 8I) helps family members to visually
identify current situations brought about by the divorce and
the effects of these changes on each family member.

The following process occurs: identify the change; the change
affects everyone in the family; the visual identification
promotes a realistic understanding and acceptance which
reduces anxiety and blame often accompanying change; it helps
family members to conceptualize the ongoing situation and
determine what actions need to be taken; and it provides an
excellent model for parents and children to recognize.

Instructions for Home Assignment:

Ask members to complete chart using the example as a guide.
Discuss the purpose of the chart using above content.
Allow time for members to ask questions. Stress that each
person's situation is unique.

HANDOUTS
FOR
SESSION 4

CHANGING SITUATIONS FOR FAMILY MEMBERS AFFECTED BY DIVORCE

Situations	Identify a specific situation in your family	How does it affect				
		Custodial Parent	Child	Child	Child	Non-custodial Parent
Example: Finances	split income	if mother, she must go to work	must buy own clothes with baby-sitting money	son cannot go to hockey camp	must consider state univ. instead of private college	reduces living standard, living in small apt.
Finances						
Responsibilities						
Time						
Space						
Relationships with Other Persons						
Visitation						
Custody						
Other						

SESSION 5

SESSION 5

BRIEF OUTLINE

OBJECTIVES: To identify specific concerns that occur in the divorce triangle between children and both parents; define how these concerns affect the children; and define alternatives for dealing with these concerns in order to strengthen family relationships.
To help parents become aware of the importance of gender identity for children and identify how others can be helpful as role models.
To illustrate the effect of parents' dating behavior on children.
To evaluate and summarize the workshop.

I. OPENING THE SESSION

A. Open Discussion
B. Brief Overview of Session

II. THE DIVORCE TRIANGLE

A. Mini-lecture
B. Exercise
C. Discussion

III. MINI-LECTURE--SELF-WORTH IN THE DIVORCE TRIANGLE

IV. SIGNIFICANT OTHERS AS ROLE MODELS

A. Exercise
B. Discussion

V. PARENTS' RELATIONSHIPS WITH PERSONS OF OPPOSITE SEX

A. Mini-lecture
B. Exercise
C. Discussion

VI. OTHER ISSUES

A. Children's Reactions
B. Visitation Issues
C. Desire to Live with Other Parent
D. Blended Families

VII. EVALUATION OF WORKSHOP

HANDOUTS

SESSION 5

I. OPENING THE SESSION

A. Open Discussion

B. Brief Overview of Session

II. THE DIVORCE TRIANGLE

A. Mini-lecture

"In a family where divorce has caused separation of the members, the challenge is to make the relationships between those family members as strong, harmonious, and growth-producing as possible. This applies specifically to the child who is caught in the middle of the divorce and feels torn in loyalty and love between mother and father; regardless of which parent has custody.

"Earlier we discussed children's feelings about the divorce and the fact that they may feel very conflicted about being loyal to both parents. One of the results of this conflict is the divorce triangle--mother, father, children. Many of these confused feelings are brought about by the parents' feelings about each other. These negative feelings are transmitted to the children, because the ex-spouse is not available to receive them. The children may feel they are being put in a position of having to take sides with one parent or the other. This can occur when children keep hearing negatives about the other parent, or feel that they are caught in the middle concerning their loyalties and who is 'right' and who is 'wrong'.

"One of the reasons that brought you to this group is your need to resolve some of the issues brought about by the nature of this triangle. The impact of these issues can have many effects on your children. Although it sometimes is not possible to change the situation that caused the issue, it is possible to determine how the situation may affect your children and ways you might handle the situation to help your children accept it.

Some of the skills that we have already discussed can help you in these situations."

B. Exercise
1. Objectives
   To help parents recognize what situations can cause discomfort to children caught in the divorce triangle. To help parents develop skills in responding to children to make them feel more comfortable in this situation.

2. Ask participants to remember a specific situation within the last month when their children returned from visiting the other parent or when their children had been visiting them.

   "Recall the conversation between you and your children regarding the specific situation. Particularly recall your response when any reference was made to the other parent. Close your eyes and put yourself in your child's place. How do you think your child feels about the response he received from you?"

   NOTE: The following questions can be discussed in the large group or in smaller groups depending on the composition of the particular group. Sometimes members work best and feel more free to speak out in small groups. Divide the participants into small groups if they function best in that way. If not, discuss the questions with the entire group.

   "How did this response affect your relationship with your children at that time?

   "Could this response have been improved to make the children feel it was okay to be with the other parent and you can accept the visit? If so, give an example of another way you could have responded to the child."

C. Discussion
   If necessary, reform larger group.
   1. Focus on the types of responses which make a child feel it is okay to like both parents, feel affection for both, and want to spend time with both. The issues should be used only as examples leading to

88

responses and feelings related to the situation.
2. Option (can be used instead of discussion or in
    addition to it):

    Role play a situation provided by parents in which
    different responses can be tried and their effect
    on child can be observed. For example:
    a. The child comes home happy after a day spent with
        Dad. Dad brings the child home late. Mother is
        upset, and annoyed at the father, knowing it
        will be difficult to settle the child in bed,
        and gets angry at the child.
    b. Hoping things are going badly since he/she has
        left, the noncustodial parent is anxious to know
        what is happening at home, whether the other
        parent is dating, how he/she is feeling. He/she
        starts asking the child a number of questions in
        a prying, demanding way. The child withdraws
        and becomes sullen; the parent gets angry.
    c. Have group members suggest situations.

III. MINI-LECTURE--SELF-WORTH IN THE DIVORCE TRIANGLE

"The reactions of parents influence how children respond to
each parent. If reactions are negative, children may feel a
conflict of loyalty to both parents. The nonadversary,
neutral approach by both parents is helpful in making children
feel good about themselves and their relationships with each
parent.

"How a parent makes reference to the other parent has direct
bearing on how children feel about their sexual selves.
Negative messages given by one parent about the other may be
translated as the 'badness' of that particular sex, which
children may then internalize as relating specifically to
their selves. Again, the child is put in the triangle.

"For example:

    "When a male child hears bad things about his father, it
    is difficult for him to believe that maleness is good,
    and if he has trouble feeling that maleness is good he
    may then have difficulty feeling good about himself.

"The same type of reaction applies to a female child.
When she hears negatives about her mother she may feel
that femaleness is not good and may then have trouble
feeling good about herself.

"When a boy hears bad things about his mother, he may
begin to distrust all male-female relationships, having
received a distorted picture of that type of relationship.
This may then affect his ability in developing a
meaningful relationship with a female later in life.

"The same applies to a girl who continually hears bad
things about her father; it becomes difficult for her to
see that a male is desirable. She may get a skewed
picture of what males are like, building a foundation
for unhappiness with males later on.

"These feelings may be compounded when children do not have
the opportunity to experience a model of an ongoing, positive
male-female relationship.

"Part of the problem of expressing negative feelings about
the other parent is that it gives mixed messages. We have
discussed the need to be aware of giving negative messages
about the 'badness' of the male or female and relating it
specifically to the father or mother. The opposite of that
is to gloss over all the bad problems that have occurred,
'Daddy/Mommy is great', is unrealistic. The children lived
with both parents through the trauma of separation. Even if
the children heard and saw very little of what happened they
know that mother and father separated; so, if everything was
all right there, then they begin to believe that they must be
to blame. It is important to be honest about both the good
and bad points of each parent. For example:

"Yes, Daddy did drink a lot and couldn't hold a job,
but he was well liked by his friends when he wasn't
drinking.

"Yes, Mother felt she had to leave home to spend some
time alone.

"This approach is far more beneficial for a child than a
negative attitude of one parent toward the other. Anytime
children are asked to turn their back on and renounce either

of their biological parents they run a major risk of
developing low self-esteem. In doing so, they feel bad, and
primarily because they are disloyal to one parent. Parents
can help children accept both the negatives and positives of
both parents by explaining that people are made up of many
different parts and in relationships sometimes two parts do
not work together. Emphasize that no one is perfect. It
helps to illustrate drawbacks, perhaps using yourself as an
example.

"I can't swim but I certainly hope you will learn to.

"I can't get along with Daddy, but you certainly can and
I hope you two will continue to have a good relationship.

"Once again it is important to emphasize the positive, because
when you stress the negative, you run the risk of damaging
children's self-esteem, for they naturally identify with
both parents in order to satisfy certain needs.

"Give children the freedom to love whom they want. This goes
back to feelings about the noncustodial parent and the need
to have positive feelings about both parents. The children
may feel they cannot love that parent and if they do they
may get into trouble. They need to be convinced that they
have that freedom. Parents can give that permission or lack
of it through subtle and not so subtle messages. For
example:

"Your father certainly got you home late tonight, and
you have school in the morning. Look at you, you're
all dirty. And where did you get that airplane? Your
father throws away his money on toys for you when I'm
stuck here without enough to go to the movies.

"I'm glad you had a good weekend with your father. Now,
hurry up and get ready for bed. You have school in the
morning.

"It is possible for both men and women to set aside their
personal feelings about their ex-spouse and express healthy
accepting attitudes concerning the opposite sex in general
(without referring to the ex-spouse) to their children. In
doing so, parents can make a concerted effort not to pass on
negative feelings toward the opposite sex to their children.

91

Sometimes, when the stress is great for the children or they feel caught in the middle it may be helpful for them to have some adult other than a parent to help them reaffirm themselves as important people. In turn, this other adult can serve as a strong role model for children, demonstrating the importance of children having the opportunity to interact with a variety of people, as a means of reaffirming their relationship with their parent and reaffirming their feelings about themselves as worthwhile individuals.

"The quality of the relationship children have with other adults determines their attitudes toward both the same sex and the opposite sex."

IV. SIGNIFICANT OTHERS AS ROLE MODELS

A. Exercise
1. Objectives
    To identify significant others who can serve as role models for children.
    To teach the importance of relationships with other adults, particularly relatives, and how these relationships can be fostered.
2. Ask members to identify those adults in their children's world who can play a significant role in their lives. List these on flipchart or blackboard.

    Examples: teacher
              religious instructor
              neighbor
              older teenage boy or girl neighbor or
                baby-sitter
              grandparents--from both sides of family
              aunts and uncles
3. "How can you foster these relationships? You might:
    a. "Invite a teacher to dinner if the child favors the idea.
    b. "Ask your children to bring friends home. This may become a reciprocal situation in which you might contact the parents of these friends and arrange for them to have the children overnight or for the weekend, or vice versa. Being with another family may provide role models of healthy mother-father, husband-wife relationships. In

addition, this family might delight in having
one or more of their children cared for outside
the home occasionally, and of course as a single
parent you can savor the luxury of time for
yourself.

    c.   "Ask adults with special hobbies (fishing, skiing,
woodworking, and so on) if they would be willing
to share some time with your children, if they
seem interested in the activity. Your relationship with this person may be 'neutral' and you
will need to feel comfortable asking a friend or
neighbor to help you.

    d.   "Let the children spend the night or the weekend
with a relative, even if it is a relative of
your ex-spouse. Often there is no problem at
all with the child-relative relationship when
parents are divorced. At other times, however,
there may be severe strains concerning birth-
days, holidays, and special occasions. It is
helpful for parents to encourage children to
maintain a close relationship through cards,
small gifts, and telephone calls even if the
parents and ex-relatives no longer get along.
As with parents, these will always be children's
relatives, despite the divorce."

B.   Discussion
In letting members share ideas for fostering other relationships, acknowledge the feelings they may be
experiencing (especially with ex-relatives) and relate
these to the children's feelings and need for positive
images to enhance self-worth. Reiterate that parents
should try to put aside their own feelings for the sake
of their children's relationships with others.

As group members share ideas about how they have included
others, or could include others in the lives of their
children, some uncomfortable feelings may be aroused or
recalled. Revealing their marital status and asking new
friends for help with their children may be very anxiety
provoking. Stomachs may start to churn as they think of
making such a request. Further, dealing with ex-
relatives may arouse other feelings; perhaps feelings
of loss, if they had been close and are now distant,
anger if they have taken sides and have been vocal,

malaise if they are unsure of the response they may get.
If, however, they are able to overcome these negative
feelings, they may be able to be very helpful to the
children.

Allow time for discussing how holidays can be observed.
Some want to maintain traditions while others want to do
things differently to help ease the pain of "remembrance
of things past."

V. PARENTS' RELATIONSHIPS WITH PERSONS OF OPPOSITE SEX

A. <u>Mini-lecture</u>

"Parents also need relationships with 'significant
others' as much as their children do, and these may well
be with individuals who have no connection at all with
the child. Formerly married adults go through a series
of stages in establishing new affectional and sexual
relationships.

"The stages may go something like this:

(1) I never want to see another man/woman. I
     don't trust any of them.

(2) Gee, that Jane (Jim) seems like a nice person.
     He (she) started talking with me at coffee
     break.

(3) Yes, I'd love to have a drink with you after
     work.

(4) Sure, we can have dinner together, but let's
     meet at the restaurant.

(5) The kids wonder where I'm going all these
     nights. Why don't you come over for dinner.

(6) Yes, this is Jim/Jane and we're all going on
     a picnic together.

(7) 'Mom/Dad is going away for the weekend
     with. . . .' This more likely occurs on the
     children's weekend with the other parent.

"It takes time for an adult to begin a new lifestyle, and there is considerable difference between the casual 'date' where there are several men/women in one's life versus the long-term intimate relationship with one person. A parent may be much further along in these stages than the children might be in accepting these varying degrees of relationships, primarily because the parent probably experienced the separation process before the children became aware of what was happening. Therefore, the children may not be as ready for the 'dating' process as their parents are. This is one reason parents may keep their relationships apart from their children, be it the casual dating process or a more serious sexual relationship. It may be difficult for the child to separate their parents as a single entity and recognize that the parent is an individual, attracted to and attractive to the opposite sex.

"There are positive aspects of a parent's dating such as the children wanting a 'daddy', or an older child experiencing relief that the parent has another interest so he/she 'will get off my back', and the parent wanting to be relieved of certain household responsibilities, or recognizing that a stepparent can also relieve financial burdens.

"There are definitely other aspects which may be confusing to the children. They may resent the idea that another person may take their father's or mother's place; they may not want to share the parent with another person; the children, having 'lost' one parent, may feel they will lose this parent as well; the children may feel like intruders in an intimate situation.

"For children becoming aware of their sexuality, the idea that their parents are sexual persons can be disturbing. For example, observing a display of physical closeness and affection between parent and 'friend' may make the children feel uncomfortable as well as making the parent feel awkward.

"Timing has much to do with how well both the parent and the children can deal with the parent's developing close relationships with other people. An awareness of the parent's closeness with another soon after the separation

95

may be disturbing to children because they may still think of their parents as a single unit, not understanding that the emotional separation possibly occurred long before. Situations such as this may provoke acting-out patterns of behavior in a child.

"How children accept a parent's new relationship depends on the comfort level of the parent in this new role. A parent who feels comfortable in his/her new relationship transmits this to the children, which helps them accept the new situation. However, when the parent is unsure of self and has ambivalent feelings, the children will sense this and react accordingly. Here is another situation in which the child may begin to misbehave to have attention once again focused on him/herself or to get rid of the parent's new friend.

"Although many issues apply to both parents, there is a difference in the effect on the children of the custodial and noncustodial parent's dating patterns. Individuals go through a series of stages in developing dating patterns, from casual to serious, and the children are eventually included in this part of the parent's life, particularly when it is the custodial parent. In this situation, it becomes part of the many changes the children are experiencing and may happen fairly smoothly because the children have access to the parent daily. When the noncustodial parent is dating and includes the 'date' on a visit from the children, the children may resent having to share their parent, they may fear losing them completely to this person and may be sad at not having that special time with the parent 'all to themselves'. The already diluted parental relationship becomes further diluted.

"The final step in the stages of developing relationships is the close, intimate sexual relationship of a parent with another who is an important part of his/her life and they want to live together but are concerned about how the children will accept the relationship. A warm, loving relationship between the parent and another may have a strong positive influence on the child. It may have been a long time since the children observed affection and kindness within the family. This display of affection may serve as a model and reaffirmation of positive family influences.

"This new close relationship will also reinforce the finality of the divorce. With the introduction of another person it becomes clear that Mom and Dad will not get back together. Because children often have a fantasy that their parents will reconcile, the bursting of this fantasy may bring about a reoccurrence of behavior seen at the time of separation. The children will again need to be reassured about the availability of both parents. You need to recognize that your children may believe that the new person is trying to 'take the place' of the other parent. As we have discussed earlier, a clear, matter-of-fact approach to the problem is required. It may be necessary to state, 'I do feel very close to Tom (Mary). I expect that he (she) will be becoming a part of our family. We will all have to learn what it will be like to add an extra person into our family. I expect that you will talk to me, or Tom (Mary) or your father (mother) when you feel you need some help. I expect that we will be talking with you when we need to'."

B. Exercise
  1. Objectives:
     To help parents determine the effect of their own affectional and sexual relationships on their children. To determine what needs to be changes to make both child/parent feel more comfortable.

  2. Divide the group in half. Ask members to think of their current dating patterns and consider the following questions together:
     How do they feel about this?
     How do they feel about their children in relation to this situation?
     What type of behavior do their children display?
     What were your children trying to say with their behavior?
     If the children do not know this individual, how do they react to your time away from them and how do you explain it?

C. Discussion

Bring group back together and ask members to comment on what they have observed about their children's reactions to their current dating patterns. You may wish to have group members examine how their children view their dating. For children younger than adolescents the dating may be seen primarily as time taken away from the child. A boy's fantasies of being "the man of the house," or a girl's fantasy of being "the lady of the house" may also be intruded upon. This may be felt most intensely if only one person is being dated. If several people are being dated, these feelings may be diluted, but confusion about who all these people are may become another issue. For adolescents, in addition to the above issues, sexual fantasies are aroused and messages about how one's own life is conducted may be inferred from the parents' behavior.

An examination of what needs the adults are trying to meet may help in understanding the child's responses. Satisfying needs for sexual gratification may be acceptable, but provocative behavior may be forthcoming from the children. Likewise, satisfying needs for affection may be mirrored by a child who may tend to cling. Understanding your needs as an adult and methods for the gratification of these needs may help in understanding your children's behavior and what need it may be serving.

"What kinds of feelings are your children displaying through their behavior?

"If the behavior is negative, what ways are there for you to modify your behavior?

"Children's reactions toward a significant other may tell the parent things about this person that the parent may not have observed. Also, children's negative feelings need not be a determining factor in whether or not the relationship is continued."

These questions and the time allowed for exploring them give parents the opportunity to weigh and set values on the pros and cons of their relationship with another and on how such a relationship affects their children.

IV. OTHER ISSUES

Following this last exercise the leaders may have time or
feel the need to discuss other issues which may have been
raised earlier in the workshop but have not been dealt with.
They may be issues that were offered by group members in the
first session but not picked up in later sessions. It is
important to be aware of these other issues (suggested topics
have been included) in order to expand them for the group's
use if they are relevant and if time allows. The issues
are presented in a manner designed to generate discussion.
This section is an "Optional Extra," and it is up to the
leader to develop it specifically for the needs of the group.

To be presented to the group and used as appropriate.

A. Children's Reactions
   1. Children may not show their feelings, but this does
      not mean they are not experiencing feelings. The
      child who pretends not to care may be so overwhelmed
      that he takes flight in silence or denial.
   2. Children should be informed as to what their parents
      are doing and planning as much as possible so they
      don't feel shut out of their lives.
   3. Children should know the arrangements for their
      support and care which is important for their sense
      of security.

B. Visitation Issues
   1. Visitation schedules: flexible or rigid?
   2. Length of visits: several short visits or one long
      visit?
   3. Using visitation rights as weapon against ex-spouse
   4. Importance of keeping appointment of planned visit;
      notify the children well in advance of change of plans

Children make own value judgments about self-worth and
the parent's feelings for them when the parent fails to
take the child for scheduled visit.

Children sometimes have plans of their own and may not
want to forfeit a baseball game or party to spend weekend
with a parent. This occurs more often as the child grows
older. Parents should recognize that this is not a
derogatory reaction toward self but a natural need for

child to be with peers and exert independence. Adjustments in visit plans will make everyone feel better.

Sometimes parents try to live within easy commuting distance of each other so that children can continue with activities in their own neighborhoods, even when staying with the other parent.

A place of their own in each of their two homes, with bureau, clothes, toys and other familiar belongings, helps children feel they "belong" in each place.

C. Children That Express a Desire to Live With Other Parent
Explore with child the reasons he or she wants to live with the other parent. This desire may be the child's way of keeping the divorce triangle interacting.
Recognize that one parent may be better for the child than the other.

A custody battle may be against the ex-spouse rather than a concern for a child's best interest. Consider the needs of the child and both parents' situations before making any changes. What the child wants may not be in the best interest of child.

D. Blended Families (Step-Families)
Blended families consist of different combinations of parents and children. While everyone involved (ex-husbands, ex-wives and children) do not live under the same roof, they are all involved in each other's lives.
Room has to be made for all of them. Each is significant to the growth and success of the members of the blended family. Many people in blended families try to live as though the other people do not exist.

In a blended family, beyond the problems of two adults living together, there are the problems that come from trying to make room for all the children involved in the new family and the other people to whom they are connected. The various interactions include: child lives with mother and stepfather; child visits father and stepmother; "her" children, "his" children and "their" children; parents' roles with own children (absent or in home) and with stepchildren.

100

VII. EVALUATION OF WORKSHOP

A. Termination

Each group leader must handle the issue of termination with the group. If the experience has been a good one, there will be some sadness. Hopefully, the group will have offered the members a positive sense of mastery of skills designed to help children and parents handle the effects of divorce in their family. This may be a time to suggest to group members that if they feel a need for further help in handling the effects of divorce they may wish some individual or family counseling to continue the work begun in the group.

B. Evaluation

The final activity of the group is to complete a written evaluation. The evaluation gives group members a chance to examine the effect of the workshop on themselves, evaluating the content and process offered by the leader. As group members complete their evaluation you may wish to discuss termination in the group or may wish to go to each member individually and comment on their participation in the workshop. The leader should expect that group members will use this opportunity to say good-bye to each other.

HANDOUTS
FOR
SESSION 5

DIVORCED PARENTS

QUESTIONNAIRE #2

I.   How were each of these expectations met in these sessions?

		Very Little	Some	A Great Deal
A.	Better understand of your children's feelings about your divorce.			
B.	Focus on how your child feels about both the custodial and noncustodial parent.			
C.	Increased understanding of how your child feels about himself.			
D.	Better understanding of how you feel about your children and your divorce.			
E.	Helping your child adjust to the role of being a "child of divorce."			
F.	Increased awareness of how divorce affects parent-child relationships.			
G.	Focus on the divorce triangle: child, custodial parent, noncustodial parent.			
H.				
I.				
J.				

2. What aspects of the workshop were <u>less</u> than satisfactory? Check
    the appropriate items listed below:

    ____ a. Opportunity the group provided to share feelings.
    ____ b. Opportunity provided to learn and share ideas and information.
    ____ c. Integration of lecture material into group discussion.
    ____ d. Amount of direction given by group leader.
    ____ e. Amount of information presented by group leader.
    ____ f. Time of meetings.
    ____ g. Participation of group members.

3. Indicate your opinion to the following statements.

                                                              YES   NO

A. I learned enough to make the group worthwhile.   ____   ____

B. There was too much lecturing and not enough
    discussion.   ____   ____

C. The series overall was helpful to me.   ____   ____

D. There was too much discussion and not enough
    information.   ____   ____

E. The group was a great help to me in dealing
    with my children and my divorce.   ____   ____

F. The objectives of the group were clear to me
    from the beginning.   ____   ____

G. I enjoyed the personal stimulation of the
    group discussions.   ____   ____

H. There was too much presentation and not
    enough interaction.   ____   ____

4. What one aspect of the group was most helpful to you? _____

    _____

5. What one aspect of the group was least helpful to you? _____

_____

6. General Comments: _____

_____

_____

_____

BIBLIOGRAPHY

BIBLIOGRAPHY

Atkin, Edity and Rubin, Estelle. _Part-time Father_. New York: Signet, 1976.

Galper, Miriam. _Co-Parenting_. Philadelphia, Pa.: Running Press, 1978.

Gardner, Richard A. _The Boy's and Girl's Book About Divorce_. New York: Bantam Books, 1970.

_____. _The Parents' Book About Divorce_. New York: Doubleday, 1977.

Grollman, Earl. _Explaining Divorce to Children_. Boston: Beacon, 1969.

Hazen, Barbara Shook. _Two Homes to Live In_. New York: Human Sciences Press, 1978.

Lietz, Theodore. _The Person_. New York: Basic Books, 1968.

Richards, Arlene and Willis, Irene. _How to Get It Together When Your Parents are Coming Apart_. New York: David McKay, 1976.

Salk, Lee. _What Every Child Would Like Parents to Know About Divorce_. New York: Harper and Row, 1978.

Sinberg, Janet. _Divorce is a Grown-up Problem_. New York: Avon, 1978.

Steinzor, Bernard. _When Parents Divorce, A New Approach to New Relationships_. New York: Pantheon Books, 1969.